PORSCHE 356

PORSCHE 356

Colin Burnham & Paul Jeffries

Published in Great Britain in 1993 by Osprey,
an imprint of Reed Consumer Books Limited,
Michelin House, 81 Fulham Road,
London SW3 6RB and Auckland, Melbourne,
Singapore and Toronto.
Reprinted spring 1997

ISBN 1 85532 677-9

Photography Colin Burnham
Text by Paul Jeffries
Captions Colin Burnham, Paul Jeffries
Editor Aimee Blythe
Page design Angela Posen
Printed in China

About the Authors

Colin Burnham is a freelance photographer/writer and the author of eight automotive
books including the highly acclaimed Osprey Colour Series titles *Air-Cooled Volkswagens*
and *Classic Volkswagens*. Paul Jeffries has worked as Features Editor for the UK's *Street
Machine*, *Classic American* and *Top Car* magazine. Both are long term admirers of the
classic Porsche 356.

Front cover
*1962 356B Coupé. The 356B was first
introduced in 1959. For 1962, the Coupé got
a taller windscreen and larger rear window*

Half-title page
*The International 356 Meeting, hosted by a
different club/country each year, is a must for
356 devotees*

Title page
*Red, white, blue or any colour you like, there's
no mistaking the venerable 356 profile*

For a catalogue of all books published by Osprey Automotive
please write to:
**The Marketing Department, Reed Consumer Books,
1st Floor, Michelin House, 81 Fulham Road, London SW3 6RB**

Contents

The 356 Story

Porsche Showcase

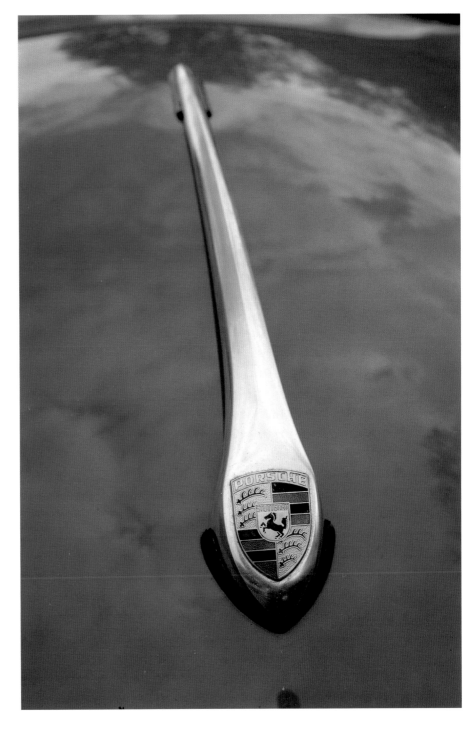

*A long, crested bonnet handle
characterized the face of the 356A*

The 356 story

More than just a number . . .

The number '356' does not exactly roll off the tongue, nor does it sound poetic. It is more the kind of random figure someone would choose if they were asked to select a number between one and 1000. Yet it is the number which, in June 1947, was bestowed on what would become one of the greatest sportscars ever produced: the Porsche 356.

This car was revolutionary – small, lightweight and agile, it was the culmination of the lifetime's work of Ferdinand Porsche. Although often thought of as German, Porsche was actually born in the Czech province of Bohemia, near Prague in 1875. From an early age Porsche had an interest in all things mechanical. His first job was in an electronics factory and later he developed an electric powered front-wheel drive vehicle displayed at the 1898 Paris World Fair – not a bad achievement for a 23 year-old.

With such talents, it was not long before Porsche was working for pioneer car manufacturer Austro-Daimler where he designed other prototype vehicles and aero engines, as well as the famous 'Prince Henry' car. His work on military vehicles and the design of an airship engine during World War I earned him an honorary doctorate from the Vienna Technical University in 1917. His 'Professor' title came as a result of being awarded the National Culture Prize, the highest civilian accolade in Germany, in 1940.

After the first World War, Dr Porsche, as he was then known, designed more cars for the Austro-Daimler company and found himself gravitating towards smaller, sporty cars such as the Sascha race car powered by a then-miniscule engine of just 1089cc. The early 1920s found Porsche working for Daimler in Stuttgart and promoted to the position of Chief Designer of the company that had now become Mercedes-Benz. Porsche's creations during that time became almost legendary and included the supercharged Mercedes Benz S series of sportscars which culminated in the 265bhp SSKL model which later won the 1931 Mille Miglia.

But for all his success in the employ of others, it seemed that Porsche was happier working on his own – or with people who thought like him. And so at the age of 56, when others might have been looking forward to a quiet retirement, Porsche made a fresh start and set up his own automotive design studio in Stuttgart. Surrounding himself with some of the best young talent he had met through his work including Karl Rabe, Karl Frohlich, Josef Kales, Josef Zahradnik, Erwin Komenda and Franz Xavier Reimspiess, the company began trading on April 25, 1931 as *Dr Eng hcF Porsche*.

It was fortunate that the venture was financed by a wealthy car enthusiast

who had the foresight to appreciate Porsche's engineering talents, as initially, business was slow. The company's first commission for a complete car was the 'Type 7' produced for Wanderer in 1931, but the engineering projects were no less ingenious or indeed, lucrative: in that same year, Porsche patented his revolutionary torsion bar suspension system and sold it to Zundapp. Later the design was bought by other vehicle manufacturers including Morris, Citroen, Standard, Triumph and ERA.

But no amount of business acumen could have predicted the effect that politics was to have on Porsche's career. The growth of fascism throughout post-war Europe, amongst other things, encouraged the idea of national superiority, and for Hitler's Nazi party it meant that German cars should be the best on the world's racing circuits. Consequently, the German Auto Union and Mercedes-Benz companies received government assistance to do just that. Porsche's involvement was with Auto Union which resulted in the technologically advanced 'P-Wagen', a 16-cylinder rear-engined racer with torsion bar independent suspension. However, the weighty rear engine caused handling problems which only the best drivers could cope with.

By now, commissions in the Porsche office were such that the company had reached project number 60. Except that Type 60 was to be more than just another job. For years, Ferdinand Porsche had been toying with the idea of a small, mass-produced but well-made car that the average German family could afford to buy and run – a concept not a million miles away from the famous Model T of Henry Ford, of whom Porsche was a great admirer. In Britain, similar ideas were afoot with Herbert Austin's 750cc Austin 7, matched in France by Citroen's 2CV.

Porsche's concept for popular transport was a small four-seater vehicle with a lightweight pressed steel body mounted on a central backbone chassis. It would be powered by a rear-mounted, air-cooled engine with integral gearbox and differential to eliminate the need for a driveshaft; the suspension was to be fully independent by means of his torsion bar and swing axle system. Although technologically advanced for the time, such a car would be practical, simple to produce and above all, cheap.

In fact, Porsche's new car for the German *volk* was not unlike the streamlined prototypes he had developed previously for German motorcycle manufacturer, Zundapp. It was even more akin to project number 32, a car he had developed for car manufacturer, NSU, which had featured a 20bhp flat-four air-cooled engine and trailing arm torsion bar suspension. Neither the Zundapp nor the NSU prototypes saw production, but Porsche believed that the concept was too good to die. And he was not the only one: Adolf Hitler, the then German Chancellor had read the biography of Henry Ford, too, and was eager for the Third Reich to be independently mobile. 'A nation is no longer judged by the length of its railway network, but by the length of its highways,' he proclaimed in 1933 during his first speech as Chancellor.

Hitler had already met Porsche when he was involved with the Auto Union race car and had been impressed with his talents, and it probably helped their relationship that they were from the same corner of the German-speaking world. So it was no great surprise that Porsche's ideas for a cheap car were enthusiastically received by the German leader and Porsche's design consultancy landed itself with its biggest commission ever: the *Volkswagen*, or 'People's car'.

The only surprise was Hitler's proposed selling price for the new car: 1000 Reichmarks – substantially cheaper than any other small car and little more than the cost of a motorcycle. The incredible pricing would be made possible by enlisting the help of the German RDA (a society of motor manufacturers) whose members would produce the components at their factories. But even with State support and Porsche's old NSU design to use as a base for the new car, many gallons of midnight oil must have been burned before the prototype Volkswagens were ready for testing in late 1935.

While Sir Malcolm Campbell, at the wheel of his 'Bluebird', was smashing the 300mph barrier at Bonneville Salt Flats in Utah, USA in 1935, the Porsche engineers had achieved a top speed of 64mph with their 984cc, 25bhp prototypes. As development continued, the cars underwent stringent tests. In 1937, 200 Nazi stormtroopers were called upon to drive one of the cars non-stop for over a million miles, in three shifts around the clock. Little wonder that with such arduous research and development, Porsche's flat-four, air-cooled 'boxer' engine soon gained a reputation for toughness and reliability.

Meanwhile, a new factory was being set up based on expertise learnt from American manufacturers. The main assembly building stretched for nearly a mile and with two shifts of workers, it was anticipated that over half a million cars would roll out of the factory each year. In the end, only 200 press and show cars were produced in 1938. Full scale production had been anticipated the following year but World War II put a brake on the 'People's car'.

During the war, only the Kubelwagen and the amphibious Schwimmwagen Volkswagen derivatives were produced. And once again, Porsche found his talents put to destructive uses with various military engineering projects including the 'Elefant' pursuit tank and the infamous V1 rocket. It was his military projects that were to prove his undoing as Porsche found himself imprisoned after the war by the occupying forces.

While Porsche was incarcerated, his son and daughter, Ferry and Louise, continued the family business in an old sawmill in the Austrian town of Gmünd, repairing agricultural machinery and constructing a rear-engined single-seater race car. Their efforts raised enough money to have the 72-year-old Porsche senior released from prison in 1947 and despite failing health during his 22-months internment, Porsche's brain had been active planning his next great project. On June 11th 1947, Porsche began his life's ambition to build a sportscar that would bear his name – The Type 356.

In 1948, overseen by Ferry Porsche, the first car gradually began to take shape in the old sawmill. It was everything that Porsche senior had wanted his sportscar to be with a lightweight, tubular spaceframe chassis clothed in a sleek aluminium two-seater roadster body designed by Erwin Komenda. Using parts smuggled in from Germany, Porsche ingeniously employed a Volkswagen engine and gearbox assembly, complete with the trailing arm suspension but mounted in reverse to make the little sportscar mid-engined. And the finishing touch must have given the old gentleman a lot of satisfaction: the name 'Porsche' on the front of the prototype 356.

Although this was Porsche's ideal configuration, perhaps because the mid-engined layout restricted cabin and luggage space, the design was taken no further. Meanwhile, a second 356 was being built alongside which had its engine and transmission mounted behind the rear wheels in the conventional Volkswagen position. Also like its Volkswagen ancestors, the second 356 featured a pressed steel chassis and floorpan. Still lacking its body, the naked 356 was road tested in 1948 and only when the team were satisfied with the car did they fit the hand-made alloy coupé body.

The curvaceous lines of the 356 prototype – which were to change little when the car was put into production – were quite a shock to many onlookers in the 1940s who were used to the more boxy style of the day. Years later, American motoring journalist M B Carroll Jr wrote: 'Wide and extremely low, almost completely devoid of chrome, this car's functional beauty grows on me. Conversely, my mother, a woman of strong opinions, refused to ride in the Porsche because of its ugliness'. But for all its critics, there were many more admirers who also appreciated the aerodynamic advantages of the new shape which had been proven using tufts of wool stuck on to the body to test its wind resistance.

Legend has it that at this time, interest in Porsche's project resulted in some advance orders from some Swiss enthusiasts, which not only paid for some of the raw materials, but also helped pay to put the car into production.

Meanwhile, the Allies had examined the Type 60 Volkswagen and, deciding that it was of no benefit to them, left the Germans to their own devices. Gradually, the Volkswagen factory began to turn out a limited number of cars and Porsche found his services were needed once again. The relationship provided not only much needed money, but of course, a continuing supply of parts for Porsche's sportscars.

But whereas the Volkswagen's 25bhp air-cooled flat-four engine was adequate for a family car, it needed a little extra zap to be of use in a two-seater sportscar. Adding twin carburettors and new cylinder heads with bigger valves and improved porting, Porsche was able to coax 40bhp from the 1131cc and 1086cc units. Each engine was carefully assembled with the pride of a skilled craftsman and stamped with the initials of the engineer.

At the 1949 Geneva Motor Show, Porsche's 356 went down a storm. People particularly liked the first production Cabriolet bodied by Beutler of Switzerland, though many were surprised at the hefty price of the sportscar compared with its Volkswagen half-sister.

Only 50 cars were made at Gmünd and Porsche production moved to Stuttgart in 1950 where some 300 cars were assembled in the corner of the coachbuilding factory that was now producing the 356 body – Reutter of Stuttgart. And there had been a few changes in the 356 since the Gmünd days. For a start, the body was now of steel instead of aluminium, and Komenda had smoothed its lines still further and added a wider windscreen and higher front 'bonnet' line.

There would be many more changes to come during the 18-year production of the 356, continuously improving Porsche's original design but never detracting from it. As the years went by, the 356 continued to notch-up victories on the race circuits while the car's classic good looks and sporty nature won praise the world over. However, worsening health meant that Ferdinand Porsche was never to see the great success of his life's ambition and he died on 30 January 1951, aged 75.

Not the car's official licence plate, but great for show

The early years: 1950–55

Little changed from Porsche's first prototypes, the 51 aluminium bodied 356 Coupés and Cabriolets with two-piece split windscreens were sold from the Gmünd factory. These early cars ran a Volkswagen engine of 1131cc which, with modified cylinder heads, valves, cam and carburettors, produced 40bhp: enough to power the sleek sportscar at speeds up to 85mph. The capacity of later engines was reduced to 1086cc to make the car eligible for the 1100cc competition class, but thanks to the expert fettling of the Porsche engineers, power output was similar to that of the 1131cc unit.

While the 356s produced at Gmünd might have appeared to be the perfect sportscars with their lightweight bodies being ideal for racing, they were, in fact, only pre-production prototypes. From the beginning, Porsche had intended his sportscar to be constructed along similar lines to the Volkswagen with floorpan and body made from steel, which was cheaper and easier to shape.

Not least of the problems was the time taken to hand-form the aluminium panels, particularly when the re-emerging Porsche company found itself overwhelmed with orders for their new car after the 1949 Geneva Motor Show. So when Porsche moved his operation to Stuttgart, the Reutter coachbuilding company took over manufacture of the 356 bodies in steel while the Porsche team got on with the business of assembling cars in another corner of the factory.

The 356 that went into production in Stuttgart was more or less what old Dr Porsche had envisaged. Erwin Komenda had made a few detail changes including subtle modifications to the roof and nose of the car, dispensing with the front quarter lights and adding a wider windscreen and a higher front bonnet line.

Underneath that smooth skin, things were similar to the prototype cars with the Volkswagen transverse-mounted torsion bar trailing-arm suspension back and front, drum brakes all round and, of course, the well proven VW flat-four air-cooled engine and four-speed transmission assembly powering the rear wheels through swing axles.

Porsche had struck a deal with the Volkswagen factory for the supply of brakes and suspension for his sportscar, while further modifications to the VW engines later in 1950 included an increase to 1283cc using piston manufacturer, Mahle's chrome-lined cylinders. Thanks to the extra capacity and better cooling, power was now up to 44bhp with top speed nudging 90mph – a very healthy speed for such a small car.

With the increased speed of the 1951 model came suitably improved braking with hydraulic operation of Porsche's own design replacing the earlier cables. Of twin leading shoe configuration, the front drums were later replaced with steel-lined alloy items for even better stopping power.

Otto Bargezi of Basel, Switzerland owns this fully restored Fish Silver-Grey early 1951 Coupé. The first 356s, with their split windscreens, skinny wheels and old-fashioned looks, hold great appeal for aficianados

Meanwhile, handling was improved with the old-fashioned lever arm dampers being replaced by telescopic items.

Operated with a short, floor mounted shifter, the gearbox was still the non-synchromesh Volkswagen unit which demanded a mastery of the technique of double-declutching for smooth gearchange. Not surprisingly, some Porsche customers were not that impressed by the transmission's harsh action and lack of synchromesh, prompting the Porsche mechanics to declare that anyone who could not make a smooth shift with the early 'crash' 'box should not be allowed to have a Porsche!

Meanwhile, the 356 was making a name for itself in competition circles with regular class wins on both road and track events. Its international competition debut had been in June, 1950 when two of the new 1100cc cars and a 1949 aluminium-bodied car entered the Swedish Rally of the Midnight Sun. Driven by Prince Furstenberg and Count Berckheim, a Coupé took the 1100cc class while the Ladies Cup was won by Countess Koskull driving the '49.

The following year, three 1300cc Porsches were entered for the Baden-Baden Rally which turned out to be less of a rally in the conventional sense and more of a high speed blast between Munich and Stuttgart. Sporting special licence plates to overcome the American-imposed 50mph speed limit, the three cars averaged 75mph for 30 hours. One of the cars was timed at an astounding 96.3mph while reported fuel consumption throughout the event was 24mpg, proving beyond all doubt the worth of the 1300 engine.

A modified Gmünd-built 356 Coupé later won its class and came 20th overall at Le Mans. But the Porsche team decided that the 356 needed yet more gusto and so the 1300cc engine was fitted with a Hirth roller bearing crankshaft which not only took the capacity up to 1488cc but blessed the engine with an ability to rev its heart out. Initially the 1500 engine produced 55bhp which soon jumped to 60bhp until a special camshaft took the power up to 70bhp.

Not surprisingly, the roller bearing crank-engined cars soon became firm favourites on the race track and few private owners worried about the extra noise of these engines. That was the sort of owner the 356 attracted: people who liked driving for its own sake, and who loved to drive hard and fast – in fact, people very similar to the competition-orientated team who designed and built the car.

But compared to other contemporary sportscars such as the British Healeys, MGs and Triumphs, the 356 was perhaps a little more refined: smoother, quieter and with suspension which actually cushioned its occupants. Thanks to the torsion bars and telescopic damping, the handling of the 356 was exceptionally precise, and compared to many other sportscars of its day the Porsche was very agile – up to a point.

The rear-engined configuration of the car meant that it was prone to sudden and dramatic oversteer when cornered at the limit which would often result in a spin if not caught in time. Many unsuspecting drivers would find themselves looking at where they had just come from; some used to joke that the best way to see where you were going in a Porsche was to look in the rear-view mirror!

However, expert Porsche drivers made cornering at the limit into an art form, developing a technique of deliberately provoking the car into oversteer and 'sawing' on the wheel as they slid around the corner. The Germans referred to their showy technique of winding and unwinding the lock as *wischen*; yet even the experts could sometimes be caught out and what became known as the 'flick roll' was the result.

British motoring writer and Porsche enthusiast, Denis Jenkinson, well remembers being demonstrated the art of piloting the 356 at high speed: he said it was easy to tell when you were cornering at the absolute limit because the movement of the suspension would be transmitted through the gearbox with the result that the gear lever would shake and flail the driver's knee!

Visitors to the 1951 Motorshow at Earls Court in London were treated to the sight of two 356 Coupés and a Cabriolet, the first German cars to be seen in England since the war. 'One of the prettiest coupés I have ever seen,' wrote another British journalist, John Bolster, in *The Autocar*.

One journalist writing for the German *Auto, Motor und Sport* liked his test car so much he could not bear to part with it: 'I can emphasize my judgement best, perhaps, by saying that in the short time that I drove this car I became so accustomed to it that I did not want to be without it and bought the test car from the Porsche firm.'

The Autocar magazine later tested a 356 and politely reported: 'It is not a car for everyone's taste, but it offers a unique combination of comfort, performance and economy for which some people will pay a very good price.' Thanks to substantial British import duties favouring domestic products, that 'very good price' was no less that £2300, when a glamourous Jaguar XK120 could be had for £1678 and an MG TD for a trifling £732. Bearing in mind that the early 356s had a wooden dipstick instead of a petrol gauge, the asking price must have seemed all the more ludicrous.

In America, the diminutive sportscars commanded the same price as a 'fully loaded' Cadillac convertible, but they struck a chord and sold well. Three 356 Porsches went to America in 1950 followed by 34 more the following year. By 1954, New York Porsche agent Max Hoffman was selling eleven cars a week.

By 1952, demand for the 356 was such that Reutter had to build a new assembly plant and the cars that rolled out of them were slightly different, too. The two-piece flat windscreen was replaced by curved one-piece glass which still retained the characteristic vee shape, while bumpers mounted further away from the body further identified the new 356. There were a few interior changes and engine options included a new 55bhp 1500cc unit with plain bearings, the roller bearing engine being designated the '1500 Super'.

There were bigger brakes, too, the 1500 Super engined cars now being capable of 100mph. But best of all was the new 'Porsche System' synchromesh gearbox. Porsche engineers had developed the baulk ring synchromesh system back in 1946 and had patented the idea and sold it under licence. With a longer gear lever, gear changes were much quicker and smoother and the synchromesh gearbox got the thumbs up from all that drove it.

A journalist from the American *Road and Track* magazine in 1952 revealed: '... after a turn at the wheel of the new Porsche and a thoro (sic) recording of test figures, one is forced to admit that *this* is The Car of Tomorrow ... It

1951–55 model 356 featuring one-piece 'vee' shaped 'screen

is safe to say that no car in the history of *Road and Track* has offered so many different and new driving sensations.'

Many years later, Robert Cumberford writing for the same magazine recalled his experiences with Porsche transmissions, new and old: 'Even with the synchro box you needed Zen-archer sensitivity to be sure of finding 2nd gear with the wavery, wobbly wand sprouting from the floor; with the crash box you needed the delicacy of a brain surgeon to find where the gear-cogs were hiding, and then a flash of brute force to slam them home.'

After all the improvements of the previous year, the 1953 cars were little changed, but perhaps Porsche was saving itself for the introduction of a new model in 1954: the famous Porsche 356 Speedster. It was a car that people either instantly loved or instantly despised due to its ultra low, bunker-effect top.

The origin of the 1954 Speedster concept is unclear, but it is certain that the enthusiastic American market had a lot to do with it. Some claim that the idea of a lightweight racer was encouraged by Hollywood, California Porsche agent, Johnny Van Neumann who had notched up numerous race wins in his alloy-bodied 356, originally a Coupé but with the roof lopped off to make it a roadster.

A few years prior to the introduction of the Speedster, Porsche produced 15 'America Roadster' versions of the 356 (with 'cutaway' doors and a split chrome-framed windscreen) which were enthusiastically received: 'The Porsche Roadster will climb up the back of a modified Jaguar XK120 up to

Early pre-'A' cars featured a radio as standard, housed in the centre of a removeable dashboard

around 70mph, and will easily outdrag a Cadillac from zero to any speed. Correctly driven, it will outcorner and outbrake absolutely anything in the genuine sports car line, anywhere near its price,' enthused John Bently in the American *Auto Age* magazine.

Others say that the Speedster was actually built at the instigation of US Porsche agent, Max Hoffman. Although the regular 356s were selling in fair numbers, he wanted something that could compete with the price of the Austin Healey and the Triumph TR2 – the Porsche's two main rivals in the American market.

Either way, the strictly two-seater Porsche Speedster was, essentially, a stripped-down, more spartan version of the regular Cabriolet for real top-down, bugs-in-the-teeth sportscar motoring which appealed to the younger market. The Speedster featured a deeper rear cowl, a removeable chrome-framed windscreen and a different dashboard. The 1488cc engine was available in two states of tune: with a 6.8:1 compression ratio producing 55bhp or a 70bhp version with a 8.2:1 ratio.

Being stripped down, the 356 Speedster was obviously cheaper to produce and sell. More importantly, it was also lighter, weighing 70kg less than the Coupé and consequently was much faster. The 356 Speedsters could run rings around their European counterparts and became an obvious choice for racing. But, even if the roundy-round circuit was not everyone's idea of fun, the Speedster's low-cut windscreen certainly cut a dash on the street and undoubtedly many enjoyed illicit competition.

With the top up, lack of headroom meant that the driver and passenger had to crouch down inside the car, though certainly in California's temperate climate, the minimalist weather gear was seldom needed. And let's face it, anyone cruising Sunset Boulevard in a Speedster wants to be noticed!

If someone was not completely sold on a Porsche Speedster the first time they were overtaken by one on the highway, then the evocative imagery of contemporary advertisements must have certainly clinched the deal: 'In terms of styling, it is the dream car of tomorrow. Crouching like a panther, as if it could take off in a mighty jump at any moment, it stands there. Its roadholding is so ideal, that even at top speed one never loses the feeling of safety . . .'

Up until this point, all of Porsche's pocket-sized performance cars had been powered by what was basically a Volkswagen engine. Though reliable, tough and surprisingly powerful, Porsche really needed an all-out race engine to establish a serious reputation in major competition. The result was the Type 547 designed by young Porsche engineer, Ernst Fuhrmann. Still with the tried and trusted air-cooled, flat-four formula, the new over-square 1498cc engine had light alloy crankcases and cylinders (with chrome bores), two spark plugs for each cylinder and a roller bearing crankshaft. With four camshafts (two per cylinder bank), two distributors, a high compression ratio and twin Solex Type 40 carburettors, Fuhrmann's engine produced 110bhp at 7000rpm.

With further modification, the 547 could produce a colossal 180bhp; but such was its complexity that it was reckoned to take a skilled mechanic around 120 hours to assemble – and one heavy footed driver a few minutes to wreck! Indeed, even its designer, Fuhrmann, is said to have estimated that it would take eight hours to set the timing. But, boy did they rev. Legend has it that a Type 550 Spyder was driven around the Sebring racing circuit at 9000rpm in third gear for hours on end after losing top gear.

It was certainly an intricate and expensive engine for such a small company, but that small company saw big rewards on the race tracks around the world. The Type 547 engine first powered the now legendary mid-engined Type 550 Spyder race car, making its racing debut at the Nürburgring in 1953 when Hans Glockler took one to a first-time win. At the 1954 Mille Miglia the Spyder won the 1500cc class and finished 6th overall. Tales from the event include one incident when a level crossing barrier dropped over the road during the race and, trusting to their car's low build, the drivers ducked down inside their cockpits and cleared the crossing barriers seconds before the train thundered by . . .

By the end of 1954 a road-going version was available. Advertised as *Der Porsche Spyder*, it was not an obvious relation to the 356 with its low lines, humped rear wheel arches, complete lack of bumpers and a windscreen which was even more skimpy than the Speedster's. It also cost twice as much as the Speedster at DM24,600. But with its power output in road-going trim now topping 110bhp for a 0–60 time of 6.2 seconds and a maximum speed of 137mph, there was no shortage of customers for the limited production special. Of the 75 cars built, most were exported to America where the car achieved a degree of notoriety when actor and teen hero James Dean met his death in a Spyder 550 in 1955.

Named in honour of Porsche's successes in the gruelling 2000-mile Carrera Panamericana Mexican road race in 1954, when Hans Hermann in his 550 Spyder came 3rd overall and won his class at an astonishing average speed of 97.6mph, Porsche introduced a Carrera version of the 356 road car. Launched at the Frankfurt Show in 1955 alongside an up-dated range of 356 models, the car was named the '1500GS Carrera'. It boasted the four-cam Spyder engine and was available in Coupé, Cabriolet or Speedster form.

Having reached 60mph from a standstill in 8.7 seconds and 100mph in 19 seconds in his Porsche Carrera GT Speedster, American journalist John Bently declared: 'what a magnificent machine – what an enthusiast's dream is this GT Carrera! It is in a class by itself.'

A contemporary American advertisement for the Porsche Carrera persuaded any last doubters to reach for their chequebooks: '5000

The original pre-suffix 356 Coupés are characterized by a more bulbous appearance, with smaller rear glass and less trimmings

kilometers straight across Mexico: many 100km long straight stretches along the Pacific at subtropical temperatures, tightly curved mountain roads at 3000 meter elevations through eternal snow, an asphalt road in the sand-polluted air of the Mexican desert! Porsche cars started here three times in the last few years. Three times they were able to score class wins, and yet more: they were able to move forward, past cars with two and three times their engine size . . . That is why 'Carrera' became the name for the crowning model of the varied Porsche program, the Type 1500GS.'

Slightly detuned for road use, the 547 engine in the Carreras had a lower compression ratio and repositioned distributors for easier maintenance. However, what was still basically a race engine was not always happy on the road, particularly in slow traffic when the engine suffered spark plug oiling. One owner describing the chore of changing the almost inaccessible plugs said that not only did it require special tools but also 'the dexterity of a trained octopus and the tenacity of a leech.' Porsche later advised Carrera owners not to drive the car at less than 2500rpm except for brief periods . . .

Goodbye vee-screen, hello 1600

Also available in the 356 range from late 1955 was a new 1600cc engine with the option of the 'S' state of tune, the lowly 1100cc engine having being dropped the previous year. All the 356 models now benefited from improved suspension including an anti-roll bar and new wheels which were one inch wider and an inch smaller in diameter. Such a list of changes resulted in the late 1955 (1956 model year) cars being designated the 356A which were easily recognised by the new constant curve windscreen instead of the characteristic vee-centred type of the previous models.

In fact, Porsche were continually making detailed improvements to the 356. Stronger gearbox mountings were introduced when it was found that enthusiastic driving led to breakage. Better brakes, upgraded dampers and thicker anti-roll bars were added while road wheels were made stronger. The flexing of the earlier wheels during hard cornering meant that loss of hubcaps was common. It was easy to spot the hard driven cars by their lack of wheel embellishment; many drivers tired of continually stopping to retrieve errant hubcaps dispensed with them all together.

High rates of import duties and tax made the 356 too expensive for many British buyers, but nonetheless highly desirable. 'Partly because an engine of modest size that provides three figure speeds and outstanding acceleration always wins affection, the superbly controllable Porsche brings back to motoring some of the joy that those privileged to drive sports cars in the earlier spacious days, must have experienced. At the wheel one feels to be one up on the other fellow in all things that matter in driving for its own sake,' laboured *The Autocar* in 1956.

Motor Sport columnist, Denis Jenkinson, bought his left-hand drive Porsche 356A in 1955 and drove it in competition events as well as touring extensively throughout Europe. Although right-hand drive cars were available in Britain, a left-hooker must have made driving on the Continent much more enjoyable. It also allowed the driver to perform 'party pieces' to impress his passengers, such as changing from third to fourth gear using his right foot to move the gear lever and his left to press the clutch.

Of course, there were disadvantages and Jenkins remembers an incident when the Porsche's lack of a transmission tunnel to separate driver and passenger nearly resulted in disaster: his passenger leant over the back of her seat to retrieve something from the rear of the car, bracing her foot against the bulkhead – or rather his foot against the accelerator pedal! Luckily, he was able to switch off the ignition before things got too out of hand.

Just like the stylish American Corvette sportscars of the Fifties, the Porsche 356 for 1957 featured exhaust tailpipes exiting through the rear bumper over-riders. Other changes in September of that year included the discontinuing of the 1300cc engine option and the use of cast iron for the cylinders which was cheaper and quieter in use than alloy. Some modifications to the clutch and gearshift completed the mechanical changes.

In addition to the appearance of vent windows on the Cabriolet, an easily removeable hardtop was offered for the model which allowed much better rear vision compared to the rag top. The Carrera was now available in Deluxe form with a better heater and different carburettors; or in lightweight GT form with a bigger fuel tank, bigger brakes and, in true sportscar style, no heater!

For the 1958 model year, the coachbuilders Drauz were contracted to build the new, better-equipped Speedster which consequently became known as the 'Convertible D'. Its taller windscreen and increased headroom must have been well received, particularly by the taller Porsche enthusiasts. Yet with proper wind-up windows in place of the side curtains, the new car never achieved the same following as its predecessors and was somewhat scorned upon by Speedster purists. Perhaps in deference to this, the 1960 model was re-named the 'Roadster' – though it did not improve sales. Only 246 Roadsters were sold in 1962, its final year of production.

No hubcaps, will travel: Hard-driven 356s tend to lose hubcaps, so enthusiastic drivers often leave them at home

The rapid Carrera GT, meanwhile, gained aluminium doors, bonnet and engine cover. Plain bearings replaced rollers in the engine but an increase in bore size to produce 1587cc resulted in 115bhp at 6500rpm. Later, the Abarth Carrera, a sleek aluminium-bodied special masterminded by Ferdinand Porsche's old friend, Carlo Abarth, should have been the pinnacle of Carrera 356 development. However, although the Abarth Carrera was built solely for the race track, it was not a great success. The aluminium *carrozeria* may have had great weight savings on the regular 356 but the car did not handle as well as expected and so the Abarth cars were discontinued after the first batch was completed.

A facelift for '59

After nearly 29,000 356 and 356A Porsches had rolled out of the Stuttgart factory, the company decided it was time for a facelift. The resulting 356B appeared in September, 1959, sporting re-designed front end sheetmetal with raised headlights and larger, higher bumpers for a more contemporary look. Other distinguishing exterior features included a larger chromed hood handle, thinner trim beneath the doors and the re-appearance of front vent windows on the Coupé.

Radial tyres now came as standard, while under the skin the 356B also boasted more rear seat legroom, a dished steering wheel and a gearbox with improved synchromesh operated by a shorter gearshift. The previous 1600 and 1600S engine options were joined by a 1600S-90 version, the '90' relating to the amount of horsepower available.

This translated into speeds approaching 115mph for the Coupé and the Roadster, as the Convertible D was now called. In line with the greater performance, all models gained finned aluminium brake drums for better cooling. Handling on the Super 90 model was also improved with a special compensating spring on the rear suspension which acted like a roll bar.

However, the American *Sports Cars Illustrated* magazine tested a 1600 Carrera Deluxe and found that generous use of the revs was needed for best performance, concluding that the earlier 356A cars were faster. Regarding the new (standard equipment) Michelin 'X' radial tyres, the testers found that they lessened the Porsche's characteristic oversteer at the expense of understeer which they described as 'formidable'. But perhaps the new tyres demanded a different driving technique.

As for creature comforts, the normal heating system of warm air ducted from the engine and forced into the passenger compartment was rarely sufficient in colder climes. Thus a 'South Wind' heater was made available. It fitted in the front luggage compartment and burned petrol to keep the

1962 Karmann-bodied 356B Coupé in eye-catching Champagne Yellow

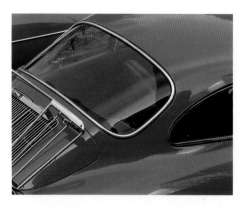

1962 and later models sported larger front and rear glass

occupants warm. Maybe it stank like a Zippo lighter and certainly fuel consumption increased with the heater on, but it was undoubtedly appreciated by many on bitter winter days.

On the subject of engine heat, although all the Porsche engines sported a huge enclosed fan to drive cooling air around the finned cylinders, it was the engine oil which did much of the cooling. Care of the oil cooler and frequent oil changes were therefore an essential part of Porsche ownership. Confident in the knowledge that their engines had withstood arduous testing and merciless thrashing on the race track, the Porsche company told its customers that they could drive flat out on the autobahn as long as they liked. But careful owners kept a close eye on the oil temperature gauge.

Although the silhouette of the 356 remained virtually unchanged throughout production, detail changes helped to keep the car looking fresh and new. With the arrival of the '62 model in September, 1961, the bodyshell received its last major modifications with an enlarged windscreen and rear window for improved visability, plus a new engine cover with two cooling grilles. Also the front bonnet received a squared-off lower edge while slightly more luggage space was made available beneath it by re-designing the fuel tank.

Even better, the new 70-litre tank could be filled via a flap in the right-hand front wing, released from inside the car. Earlier models had to be re-fuelled from underneath the bonnet which often meant that luggage got soaked when making gas stops in inclement weather – not to mention the risk of spilling fuel on it at all other times! Another problem encountered in garages related by Denis Jenkinson was that as the chrome lifting handle on the bonnet grew longer with each 356 re-style, so it became more susceptible to heavy-handed forecourt attendants who would bend them trying to close the lid.

Sadly, 1962 also meant goodbye to the appealing machismo of the Porsche Roadster but the day was saved with the appearance of a new, even more powerful Carrera. Powered by a 2-litre version of the four-cam engine and known as the Carrera 2, this was to be the last of the 356-based Porsche Carreras. Shown at the Frankfurt Motor Show in 1961, the Carrera 2 did not enter production until the following year, but with its 130bhp 1996cc engine, it was the ultimate road going Porsche. It could reach 60mph from a standstill in less than eight seconds and top over 125mph with more than its fair share of panache.

With detailed graphs showing performance and fuel consumption, pictures of the car from all angles and even an illustration of the 2-litre, four-cam engine, brochures for the Carrera 2 were clearly aimed at the most serious high performance car enthusiast. The text aptly described the highly strung machine as a 'race horse tamed by a master's hand'.

While the standard 356 was made suitably comfortable for the sporting driver and passenger with reclining front seats, rear seat passengers were comfortable only if they were small children – the limited space in the rear of the car was better used for stowing luggage.

Even with the purpose-built Porsche suitcases sold as extras, the 356B's front luggage compartment was still all-too limited compared to other cars. A useful accessory and something of a necessity when touring was the rear-mounted luggage rack. Other accessories for the proud Porsche owner included such things as an anti-glare mirror, special floormats and an electric sunroof. The ultimate style accessory, however, had to be a set of pierced chrome wheels.

Compared to some cars, the accessory list for a 356 was somewhat limited. Porsche claimed that this was because most of the fittings that were extras on other cars at the time were standard on theirs. For example, apart from useful devices such as variable speed windscreen wipers, the existing door and ignition locks on a 356 were supplemented with a gearshift lock fitted as standard for extra security. A radio, however, was still an optional extra – perhaps they considered that most owners would be content listening to the delightful sound of the flat-four engine behind them!

Also available in 1961 was the officially named 'Hardtop 61'; basically a Cabriolet with a steel hardtop welded in place. The actual hardtop, made by Karmann, had previously been offered in 1957 as a removeable option for Cabriolets and, as such, made a good deal of sense. The 'permanent' Hardtop 61, however, was not especially well received; around 1700 examples were produced during its two year run.

Little more than ten years since the fledgling car company started producing its revolutionary sportscars, Porsche's production history stretched back over some 40,000 cars. By this time, the demand for Porsche bodies proved too much for both the Reutter and Drauz coachbuilders to cope with, so manufacture of the Reutter Coupé bodies was shared by the Osnabrück-based Karmann company while production of the last Roadster shells was completed by D'Ieteren of Belgium.

So what was it that made this diminutive but costly sportscar such a great success? A Porsche advertising brochure told prospective customers what Porsche owners had been saying for years: 'How does one explain this unique fascination that is exuded by the Porsche name?' it asked, and went on to trumpet the attributes of the 356. Its 'functional beauty', the 'harmony of the technical equipment' and 'the already proverbial good roadholding and the inspiring spirit of the powerful motor'; adding the testament of one satisfied customer for good measure: 'There are many good cars, many good names, but only one Porsche.'

Playboy author, Ken W. Purdy described the Porsche's superior attributes in more evocative, tangible terms. The Porsche, he wrote, '. . . delivers more sheer sensual pleasure than anything else on wheels . . . The available acceleration is astounding . . . a Porsche driver sits there, clipping through holes in the traffic pattern that just aren't there for anybody else, and, when he wants to, running away from almost anything he sees.'

'The transmission works as smoothly as a spoon of molasses and you can slam it back and forth from gear to gear just as quickly as you can move your hand . . . The brakes are about 50% oversize and air-cooled beyond possibility of fade; and the steering, very soft and very quick, is what power steering tries to be and is not.'

'The seats are contoured to reach around and hold you gently at the hips and shoulders. Driving a Porsche, you can, with small effort, believe that the seat of your trousers is part of the automobile,' he concluded.

And it was not only the 356's stylish good looks that won favour with the ladies. Recounting her first trip behind the wheel of a 356B convertible, Trudi Dembi wrote in the American magazine, *Popular Imported Cars*: 'I remember being stunned by the all-of-a-sudden recognition of the pleasure of driving the Porsche. It turns at a thought. Shifting up or down is effortless and one finds oneself playing with the gearbox for the fun of it. My confidence in driving in traffic, on the highway . . . and in parking too, all overwhelmed me within the space of the first few minutes of that beautiful day.'

The final development

It was only in 1963 when nearly 60,000 Porsche 356's had taken to roads all over the world that the first 'pure' Porsche was made – the 356C. That is not to say that the previous models were lesser cars, rather that 1963 was when Porsche finally began manufacturing its own bodyshells, having bought out the Reutter coachbuilding company.

By this time, the basic lines of Porsche's smooth, flowing, aerodynamic body had remained virtually unchanged for nearly 15 years. When it first appeared, people either loved or hated its revolutionary shape – and it was still causing a stir by the mid-sixties, as *Canada Track & Traffic* reported: 'There had been cause for dispute about the early styling of the Porsche. To some it was pure and pretty, but to others, particularly those who like fins and squared lines, the Porsche resembled a turtle with wheels . . . The current model, in our opinion, is a welcome curvaceous relief in these days when most bodies are basically box-like.'

The Porsche 356C, introduced in the summer of 1963, was basically a 356B bodyshell but with disc brakes on all four wheels as standard, and easily distinguishable from its drum braked brethren by its flat hubcaps. Designed by Porsche and built by the Dunlop subsidiary, ATES, the four wheel disc

The 'C' featured disc brakes on all four wheels along with re-designed front wheels (chrome optional) and flat hubcaps

brakes with handbrake drums built in to the rear discs were a great success, leading one motoring magazine to say that they were among the best they had tested.

Some considered Porsche's adoption of disc brakes a little tardy, especially for a high performance sportscar. After all, other, cheaper family cars had featured front disc brakes since 1960. However, the Australian *Sports Car World* thought that 'This was probably because Teutonic thoroughness would not entertain disc brakes without an efficient handbrake; so they built a small drum brake into the rear discs to do the job.'

Other improvements which marked out the 356C included a removeable rear window on the Cabriolet and a shorter gearshift on all the cars. As for motive power, standard engine options for the new model were limited to the 75bhp 1600C (The Super 75 model) and the 1600SC; the most powerful pushrod engine producing 95bhp. The potent 1996cc Carrera 2 unit provided owners with various power outputs according to its state of tune, from a relatively staid 88bhp to a neck-snapping 130bhp. Interestingly, one American Porsche agent found the basic 88bhp car was able to out-drag its more muscular SC counterpart – but only up to a point.

Reporting back on his 356C 1600SC, Frank Coggins of the American magazine *Popular Imported Cars* suggested a new marketing ploy: 'Surprisingly, we got some great kicks out of the car, of all places, right in the midst of Manhattan traffic on Third Avenue during the rush hours. Here, the lovely, quick steering and that fabulous acceleration took so much of the bore out of working our way uptown that it was about the best thing a salesman could do to push the car to a prospective customer.'

Porsche's four speed synchromesh gearbox came in for high praise from all who handled it. 'Movement is short, yet always into the desired cog. Fast as the hand can move, it's nearly impossible to beat the synchro,' sang one journalist, adding that he once selected reverse by mistake while racing his Porsche. Apparently, the engine was blown to smithereens but the gearbox was fine.

Adjustable Boge telescopic shock absorbers fitted as standard improved handling considerably and many owners fitted similar dampers to earlier cars. *Canada Track & Traffic* were so impressed with the development of the 356C's suspension that they declared: 'Porsche orientated drivers are in for a delightful surprise when they climb behind the wheel of a 356C. Roadability is amazing for this rear engined car and oversteer is gone . . . at least to the point of really fast cornering,' enthused the writer. 'Until extreme cornering speeds are reached, the Porsche handling remains neutral. Combined with the lightness of the steering it makes cornering a delight, even for the novice. The transition to oversteer is gradual, and when reached permits the car to be drifted in classic fashion.'

In either Coupé or Cabriolet form, the 356C was undoubtedly the most sophisticated and well equipped of all the Porsches with its excellent brakes, agile handling and lusty 1600SC engine. But there seemed to be a growing feeling among some that the 356 was perhaps getting a little long in the tooth. The spartan dashboard, for example, which had earlier been praised for its functional simplicity was now being criticised by some journalists who probably felt that a painted metal dashboard was not becoming on a car of that ilk – or price.

It would be all-too sentimental to think that Porsche were content with the 356C, feeling, like the writer in *Canada Track and Traffic*, that it could not be bettered: 'The Porsche, developed for more than a decade, has reached a plateau of near perfection . . . Porsche offers comfort and old world quality along with race bred performance . . . Its limits are largely those of the driver.' In reality, the Porsche staff were devoting all their energy to the 356's replacement, the 911. The project had been underway for some time and the new 911 bore a striking resemblance to the 356 – though of course, it was to receive a six-cylinder air-cooled engine.

By the late summer of 1964, the 911 was in production but problems with the new car forced the company to allow the much loved 356 a stay of execution. Part of the reason was that the company was reluctant to lose sales of its affordable base-model 356 to the more expensive 911. Only when a budget version of the new car, dubbed the 912, appeared in April, 1965 did production of the venerable 356 come to a close. In September, 1965, after 17 years of production, the last Porsche 356 quietly rolled off the Stuttgart production line.

But it was not quite the end of the car. Ten more 356s were later built as special orders, such was the following of Porsche's original sportscar.

Epilogue

As with many cult cars, each Porsche number has its own devotees; but there seems to be something quite special about the 356 that even non-car enthusiasts are captivated by its charm and style when they would not even give one of the more muscular and spectacular 911s a second glance.

Writer Denis Jenkinson remembers driving one of the new 911s and came away decidedly non-plussed. It was bigger, had softer springs and rolled more; and that apart from its being much more complex than its predecessor. Jenkinson had always marvelled at just how much the diminutive Porsche could do for its size.

The 356 is, without doubt, the prettiest, most stylish and charismatic car ever to roll out of the Porsche factory and, as Jenkinson believes, probably set the standard for post-war sports and GT cars. But there is something else that makes the 356 a classic: a presence or feeling which most other cars just do not have.

Comparing a 356 Speedster with its 1990 911 counterpart, John Lamm, writing in the American *Road & Track* magazine said that whereas the 911 Cabriolet was: '... slacks, a cashmere V-neck, Gucci loafers and a power-operated top. The Speedster is Levis, cable knit sweater, old sneakers and fold your own. It feels as though you're supposed to smile with contentment in a Cabriolet. You get to laugh in this one. Speedsters do that to people.'

In a similar vein, Peter Bohr for the same magazine: 'Now why would anyone pay twice the price of an early Porsche 911, with all its performance, comfort and handling advantages, for an aneamic-performing, quirky handling and relatively cramped car that looks like an overturned bathtub ... Because for all their shortcomings, Porsche 356s are downright lovable.' Amen.

At home on the road: Speeding along the highways and byways of Britain in a red Speedster is surely the most fun you can have on four wheels

Porsche Showcase
Thoroughbred Coupés

Right
More than 40,000 Coupés were produced between 1950 and 1965. Here are a handful of right-hand drive models that have survived the unforgiving British climate

Overleaf
David Foster's fully restored 1960 356B Super Sunroof, one of the first of the 'facelift' models

30 year-old David Foster from Surrey, England bought his first 356 after reading a magazine article about the model, and within a short time Porsche dealing became a full-time occupation. Needless to say, most of his stock comes from sunny California . . .

Left
View through the optional steel sunroof. Compared to modern-day sportscars, the 356 interior is somewhat basic – but then this was a car that was designed with the 'sporty' driver in mind

Below
Exhaust outlets were first incorporated within the bumper guards in late '57, a move which proved none too popular amongst many buyers who soon tired of wiping soot from the chrome

Above
One of the last 356s to roll off the
production line sporting a rather
appropriate British number plate

Right
Early vee-screen Coupé hails from
what was the 'other' side of the fence
in Germany, reputedly the only daily-
driven 356 in the old Eastern Block

Above
Seven times 356 Coupé equals one impressive line-up

Right
Memorabilia: Perhaps in years to come these plaques will be as sought-after as the car they commemorate

Previous page
Dr Porsche's renowned air-cooled flat-four grew from its original 1131cc to almost 2-litre capacity during the evolution of the 356. This is a late Fifties standard 1600cc version with 60bhp at 4500rpm

Left
Well-earned wash: One of the many German owners who drove to northern England for the 1991 Internationals prepares his car for the Concours d'Elegance at Harewood House

Below
The hardtop's slippery fastback styling remained virtually unchanged throughout the car's 17-year history

Above
Three of a kind but each unique to their respective owners

Right
Participants in the 1991 356 Internationals in Yorkshire were given the opportunity to blow the cobwebs from their cars on the Harewood hillclimb circuit. Much enjoyment was had by all

Right
The 1960–63 Porsche 90 was fitted with a 90bhp 1600S engine, sufficient to propel the Coupé to 115mph and deliver 'more sensual pleasure than anything else on wheels', as Playboy writer Ken W. Purdy enthused at the time

Below
From Stuttgart to stoplight in old Harrogate – but the pedestrians weren't especially impressed

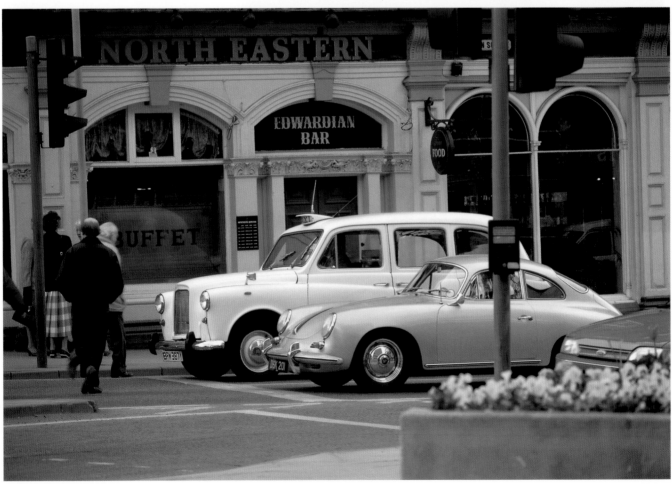

Above
Caught in action on the track

Left
High-gloss 'As, from Sweden

The 356B featured a larger chromed
bonnet handle to that of the 'A'. All
models benefitted from high quality
paint finish

1962 and later model years displayed a squared-off bonnet. Also that year, a gas filler flap appeared on top of the front wing

Left
Exterior mirrors such as this Durant-style item were optional extras on the cars when new

Below
'Beehive' rear lights, side by side, replaced the earlier vertical arrangement in the 1953 model year. 'D' is for Deutschland *or* Das Vaterland, *whichever you prefer*

Further proof of the enthusiasm for the marque

The Super model featured special hubcaps, often referred to as the 'nipple' type

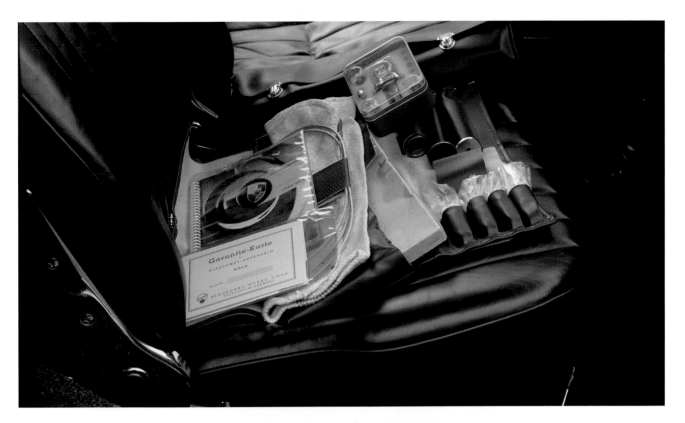

Above
Essential spares for any 356 driver

Left
Grand Tourer: Period suitcase strapped to chromed luggage rack adds a nice touch

Overleaf
Porsche posse: Part of the large German contingent pause during the 'Grand Drive of North Yorkshire' in 1991

Not an everyday sight , . . .

It has been said that the 356 resembles a 'turtle with wheels' and an 'overturned bathtub'. But of course, those who appreciate the finer things in life know better . . .

Someone once said that changing the
spark plugs on a 356 demanded the
'dexterity of a trained octopus and the
tenacity of a leech.' Here's proof!

1600S 75bhp engine, beautifully detailed. This unit was available from October, 1955, initially with a roller bearing crankshaft, and produced almost double the horsepower of Porsche's original 1131cc engine

Topless beauties

1962 right-hand drive Cabriolet is arguably the finest of its kind in Britain, a frequent show winner even at non-Porsche events

Right
Ever since the first Porsche rolled off the assembly line the cars have proudly borne the name of their creator on the rear panel. In the late Fifties, the script was gold-plated brass

Above
The Cabriolet may be better suited to the sunnier climes of West Coast America, but the snug-fitting padded top means it is equally practical on those grey European days

Low-slung headlights and corresponding metalwork denote this Cabriolet as a pre 'B' model – that is, built before September, 1959 (1960 model year). Quarter lights, or vent windows, first appeared on Cabriolets two years earlier, therefore this Dutch-registered example is either a '58 or '59 model

The Roadster was the last embodiment
of the Speedster tradition, replacing
the Convertible D in September, 1959,
though discontinued two years later

Above and overleaf
The International 356 Meeting is always a truly cosmopolitan affair. Witness this shining example of a 'B' Roadster, driven all the way from Italy

Barcelona to Harrogate takes more
than a few tankfuls of gas, but this
was the final fill-up for the Spanish
contingent before reaching their
destination. Nearest the camera is a
95bhp SC Cabriolet, adjacent is an
earlier Convertible D

Crème de la crème: Cream coloured French Cabriolet would be a cool cruiser in Cannes (or anywhere else for that matter)

Above
Brace of Cabriolets: Red 'C' type (with optional waistline trim) leads earlier 'B' over the Yorkshire Dales

Right
All action on the Harewood hillclimb circuit for this English-registered 'A' Cabriolet

Opposite
Two rag-tops bring up the rear of a lengthy, London-bound caravan following the Harrogate meeting

Left
A small gold plaque commemorating
Porsche's racing wins was placed on
the dash of open-top 356s of the late
Fifties. The miniature framed
photograph was added by the owner

Above
Wood-rimmed Nardi steering wheels
were, and are, a popular accessory for
the 356. This is the later dished type
with ebony inlay and crested boss

Above
*Period Blaupunkt radio and matching
speaker provide adequate
accompaniment for most 356 drivers.
A modern-day, mega-watt sound
system would look so out of place ...*

Right
*Three facelifts on, the dash of the
356C was a little better equipped but
remained painted metal*

Previous spread
*Hats on and ready to go. You certainly
need one in the back of a Cabriolet!*

The 1954 model year saw the introduction of horn grilles alongside the indicators, while fog lights mounted on the bumper or recessed into the nose were optional from 1955. Chrome plated bumpers are rarely seen on early models

Left
A removeable steel hardtop was offered for Cabriolets from the 1958 model year onwards. Easily removeable in a few minutes, it made the Cabriolet a genuine all-year-round car

Below
Stuttgart coachbuilders, Reutter, built the bodywork of the 356 from its beginnings until 1963, when the company was absorbed by the Porsche factory. Thus the majority of cars bear the nameplate in one of three variations on the right front wing

Right
Four into 2+2 won't go – unless the back seat passengers are into yoga!

Opposite page
Legend on a licence plate: '356' may be an anonymous number to the uninitiated, but to Porscheophiles the world over it has a magical significance

Sunday's child:
the Speedster

The Porsche Speedster differed from its 356 counterparts with its removeable, chrome-framed windscreen – although 'flyscreen' would perhaps be more appropriate

Previous spread
*Retro chic: Compared to the modern-
day Eurobox, the charismatic
Speedster is in a league of its own*

Above
*With its deep rear cowl and low-slung,
bunker-effect rag top, the Speedster is
largely considered to be the most
desirable of all early Porsches —
certainly the rare four-cam
Carrera version*

Eye-catching mustard yellow paint job on Patrick Amos's British registered '55 Speedster is definitely non-original. Ditto the car's 1600S engine and 'C' disc brakes

Rag tops down, bonnets up — let's gas-up and go!

Early Porsches here, there and everywhere – though a bright red Speedster will stand out at any automotive occassion

Above
High-gloss aquamarine finish accentuates the Porsche's multi-contoured metalwork. They don't make 'em like they used to ...

Right
'Aero' mirrors were offered by the factory during the late Fifties

Domed hubcaps were a stylish feature of all early cars. Wheel width and diameter changed from $3\frac{1}{2} \times 16$in. to $4\frac{1}{2} \times 15$in. with the introduction of the 356A in late 1955

Right
This prize-winning 1956 model, imported to Britain by Porsche specialist David Foster, is period-perfect in every respect. Moreover, if you have to ask how much he wants for the car, or one like it, chances are it's well out of your price range . . .

Below
The 'Speedster' script adorned each front wing above the waistline trim. Very early models were distinguished by a more elegant, old-fashioned script

Above

*With tonneau cover in place, the
Speedster was strictly a two-seater
with the barest of creature comforts.
Pod-type dashboard was a feature of
Speedster, Convertible D and Roadster
models only*

Right

*With its removeable tubular frame,
the 'low bow' top was standard on all
Speedsters up until mid-1957 when it
was replaced by a 'high bow' version
giving slightly more headroom. Metal-
shelled bucket seats with minimal
padding and front-mounted hinges
were peculiar to the model throughout
its four year production run*

Above

*The original horn grille, as pictured
here, was fitted from mid-1954
through 1959, when they were
modified with the introduction of
the 356B*

Previous spread
American spec cars sported bumper overrider tubes from September, 1956 onwards, while the twin vent grilles on the rear of the Speedster's bright red companion identify it as one of the last 356 Roadsters

Above
Pilot's headgear was not listed in the Porsche accessory catalogue during the Speedster era but it would have been a great seller. Belgian-registered car was built in early '57

Above
Others prefer 'sporty' caps

Overleaf
Spot the Speedsters . . .

Race track refugees

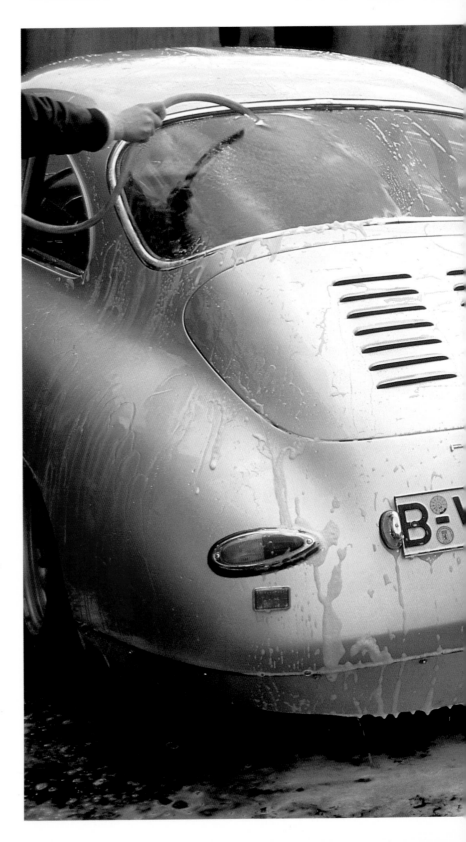

Right
With racing style louvres and a single exhaust but sans bumpers, this squeeky clean machine is just about ready for the track

Overleaf
The equivalent of the latter-day Porsche 911 Turbo, the 356 Carrera was named in honour of Porsche's triumphs in the 1953 and 1954 Carrera Panamericana road race in Mexico. It was equipped with a competition-developed four-cam engine, initially with a power output of 100bhp at 6200rpm in the 1956 1500GS, and was later developed to produce a healthy 130bhp in 2-litre form. Top speed was over 125mph in all but the earliest models, and sub-8 second 0–60 times were recorded, though the 10–11 second mark was the norm. Part of the Carrera's appeal was that apart from the subtle badging it looked identical to the standard model, be it Coupé, Cabriolet or Speedster

Left

Only ten 'A' bodied four-cam Carreras were exported in right-hand drive specification between late 1955 and August 1959. Each costing the equivalent of two detached houses in the home counties at the time, only four are known to have survived in Britain. Fred Hampton's beautifully restored '56 model is one of them

Above

Fred's 1500GS Carrera is complete with its original engine, the Type 547/1 four cylinder, twin plugs per cylinder, twin distributor, twin valve opposed engine with four overhead camshafts. Indeed, the Carrera motor had little in common with the early Porsche/Volkswagen unit

Overleaf

Wouldn't you be proud to wear the Porsche colours if you owned one of the last 126 356C Carreras built? Furthermore, wouldn't you be proud to show off its four-cam engine?

Above

The last of the 356-based Carreras, the Carrera 2 was blessed with a 1996cc capacity engine. This pumped out an honest 130bhp at 6200rpm, with its peak torque of 119lb/ft coming in at a mere 4,600rpm. Unfortunately this race engine was not happy idling in road traffic and to avoid constant plug fouling Porsche advised owners not to run their engines at less than 2500rpm except for brief periods!

Left

The last of the 1194 Carrera models built during the 356 series production featured gold-plated badging, accentuating its desirability

Above
Two of a kind: 1990 911 Speedster keeps company with Richard King's period racing-style '57 Coupé

Right
Sixties-style mirror enhances the sporting nature of the 356

Aluminium brake drums first appeared in the 1953 model year and were superceded by finned drums for improved cooling on the 356B. Four-wheel disc brakes were finally incorporated in the 356C of 1963

Pot metal headlight grilles were standard equipment on Speedsters and optional on other models in the 1955 model year. The grille was inserted in place of the lens

Alternatively, with the introduction of the 356A came the optional wire mesh grille which was installed over the lens

*Reputed to have taken part in the
legendary Carrera Panamericana
many years ago, this pre-'A' 356
created plenty of interest on Concours
day at Harrogate*

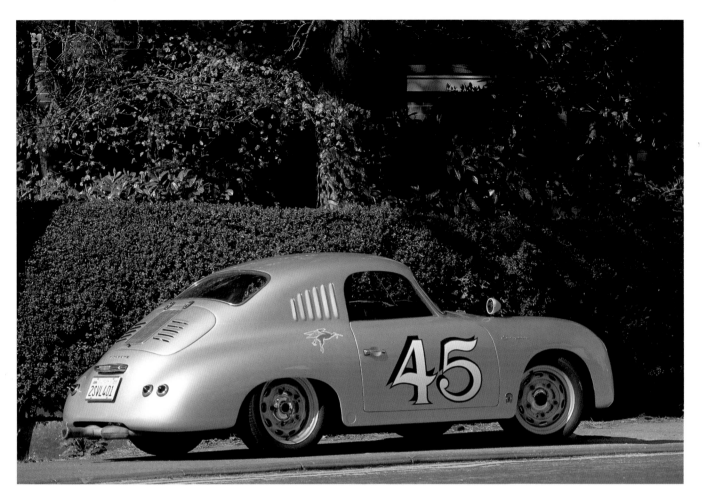

Without bumpers or hubcaps and lowered at both ends, this silver Coupé certainly looks ready for action...

With the full American competition
look, this California-built three-
window Coupé appears somewhat out
of place on English turf. It was shipped
over from the US specially for the 16th
International Meeting

Above

The rare 'European' script was attached to the fenders of a small number of 356As destined for the American market. Legend has it that these cars were 'strippers' fitted with standard engines but without rear seats and so on; variations on the no-frills Speedster theme

Left

Louvres in place of the rear side windows duct extra cooling air into the engine compartment. Polished brake drums and period decals merely enhance the old-time flavour

Racing RSK on road and track. Porsche's victories in the early Fifties Carrera Panamericana races were achieved by its specially built four-cam 550 Spyder race cars. This is believed to be the only English-registered later-model Type 718/1500 RSK Spyder, the similar looking successor to the legendary 550 introduced midway through the 1957 racing season. Some 5in. lower and 44lbs lighter than the 550, the RSK featured coil springs instead of torsion bars at the rear along with a four-cam engine initially tuned to produce 142bhp. The RSK was a highly successful machine on race tracks throughout the world

The 356 Carrera was invincible in the 1600GT competition class of the late Fifties. But fearing the challenge of Lotus and Alfa Romeo, Porsche commissioned Zagato, through his old friend Carlo Abarth, to build a run of lightweight aluminium-bodied Carreras. Thus was born the distinctive Abarth Carrera. Although visually exciting the car was not a huge success in competition, and after the initial batch had been completed the project was dropped. This impeccably restored example owned by early Porsche aficionado, Bob Garretson, was originally built in 1961, raced in Mexico until 1965, and Bob acquired it in 1970. Following its 20-year restoration (yes, twenty years!) the car was finally unveiled at the 1991 Internationals and, quite deservedly, its owner took home the 'Best of Show' trophy. Name your price, Bob

Meticulous attention to detail is displayed in every department, not least the engine compartment where the Type 547 four-cam motor thumps out almost double the horsepower of a basic 1600cc pushrod engine

The Porsche Carrera GTS, more commonly known as the '904', was built for a limited period in 1963–64. Its rakish, Ferrari-like fibreglass bodywork was styled by 'Butzi' Porsche, grandson of the founder, and it was the last competitive Porsche to use a modified road engine

Radically different from any Porsche
that had gone before, the 150mph-plus
904 led to the development of the 906,
907, 908, 910 and the glorious 917

Overleaf
Early right-hand drive Carrera;
probably the rarest of all 356 models

Specifications etc.

Throughout its life the Porsche 356 remained basically unchanged in its general conception. A wide range of engines were offered over the years, from a pushrod overhead valve 1100cc unit to a 4-camshaft 2-litre, but the basic layout of the four air-cooled cylinders, horizontally opposed in pairs and cooled by a fan, remained unchanged. Similarly, the positioning of the engine behind the rear axle (with the gearbox ahead of the axle) was unchanged from the first 1950 models right through to the 1965 Carrera GS.

Engine
Common to all 356 models. Mounted behind rear axle.

Valve gear
Inclined overhead operated by pushrods from single central camshaft mounted under crankshaft. Carrera engines have two overhead camshafts on each pair of cylinders, driven by shafts and bevel gears from crankshaft.

Cylinders
4 – horizontally opposed at 180°, in pairs.

Firing order
1–4–3–2. Cylinder numbering – 1: front right side. 2: rear right side. 3: front left side. 4: rear left side.

Fuel system
Common to all models.

Tank
Single sheet-steel tank mounted in front of cockpit bulkhead.

Capacity
52 litres (plus 5 litres Reserve). 11.5 Imp. galls (1.1 Imp. galls Reserve). 13.74 US galls. Sandard tank for 356. 80 litres (15 litres Reserve) – 17.5 Imp. galls (3.5 Imp. galls Reserve). 21.13 US galls. Carerra GT tank optional on other models from '56.

Pump
Mechanical, mounted on crankcase. Carrera models use two electric pumps mounted in nose of car.

Carburettors
Two downdraught (one for each pair of cylinders). Single choke Solex on early engines, twin-choke Solex or Zenith on later models and S models.

Lubrication
Wet sump, with oil cooler in fan housing on all pushrod engines.

Engines used in 356 series Porsche

Model	Engine type	Bore & stroke (mm)	Capacity (cc)	Compression Ratio	BHP (DIN)	RPM	0–60mph (seconds)	Max. Speed (mph)
1100	Normal	73.5 × 64	1086	7.0:1	40	4200	23.5	85
1300	Normal	74.5 × 74	1286	6.5:1	44	4400	22	90
	Super			8.2:1	60	5500	17	95
1500	Normal	80.0 × 74	1488	7.0:1	55	4400	15.5	100
	Super			8.2:1	70	5500	13.5	110
1600	Normal	82.5 × 74	1582	7.5:1	60	4500	16.5	100
	Super			8.5:1	75	5000	14.5	110
	Super 90			9.0:1	90	5500	13.5	115
	'C'			8.5:1	75	5200	14	110
	'SC'			9.5:1	95	5800	11.5	120
1500	Carrera GS	85.0 × 66	1498	8.5:1	100	6200	12	120
	Carrera GT			9.0:1	110	6400	11	125
1600	Carrera GS	87.5 × 66	1587	9.5:1	105	6500	10.5	125
	Carrera GT			9.8:1	115	6500	10	125
2-litre	Carrera GS	92.0 × 74	1996	9.5:1	130	6200	9	130

Dry sump with oil tank behind left-rear wheel on Carrera engines, with double-bodied pump for pressure and scavenge.

Cooling system

All models: air cooling by belt-driven fan in housing above engine. Air forced downwards over finned barrels and head, with exit below and behind. Bleed-off through filters for cockpit heating on pushrod models. Special twin-rotor fan on Carrera engines, delivering 39cu.ft. (1.10 cu. metres) per sec at 6200rpm.

Transmission

All models: 4-speed and reverse, mounted ahead of rear axle. Central gear lever and long rod to gearbox selector mechanism.

Gear change

H-pattern gear change, with first forward left, second backward left, third forward right, fourth backward right. Reverse far left forward after pressing lever down against spring.

Gearbox

Porsche/VW non-synchromesh on 356 models. Porsche baulk-ring synchromesh on all four gears from 1953 onwards. Eary cars had two-piece aluminium gearbox. Changed to three-piece housing in 1956 model year (356A) and to barrel-type housing with end plates in 1960 model year (356B).

Clutch

Single dry-plate. Cable operated.

Chassis and body

Steel floor pan with pressed steel welded body welded to it. Front lid hinged at rear for access to spare wheel, fuel tank and luggage space. Rear lid over engine hinged at top for access to oil filler, dip stick, carburettors, electrics etc. Valve gear accessible from under car. Front and rear lids stay up with automatic over-centre catches. Released by lifting above static position and then lowering.

Suspension

Front

Independent by two trailing arms each side. Springing by laminated torsion bars mounted transversely inside tubular cross-member. Anti-roll bar from 356A onwards. Telescopic hydraulic shock absorbers.

Rear

Independent by swinging half-axles. Tubular half-axles pivot on gearbox casing. Fore and aft location by radius plates running forward to chassis and connected to transverse round-section torsion bars inside tubular cross-member. Telescopic hydraulic shock absorbers. Transverse single-leaf compensation spring mounted under axle on C and SC models.

Steering

Volkswagen worm and peg steering box, with two-piece track-rod on 356. ZF worm and peg steering box from 1957 on, with two-piece track-rod and telescopic hydraulic damper on 356C and Carrera.

Minimum turning circle

34ft on pushrod models (10.2 metres). 36ft on Carrera models (11.0 metres)

Number of turns

$2\frac{1}{2}$

Brakes

Front

Aluminium drums with steel liners ('53 and later), ATE-Lockheed hydraulic two-leading shoe system. 356C and 356SC had disc brakes by ATE-Lockheed.

Rear

Aluminium drums with steel liners. ATE-Lockheed hydraulic two-leading shoe system, with cable operated handbrake mechanism. 356C and 356SC had disc brakes by ATE-Lockheed, with handbrake operating on shoes within small drum integral with disc.

Wheels and tyres

Pressed steel disc wheels with perforations and five stud fixing. 356: 3.25J × 16 rims. 5.00 × 16in. tyres 5.25 × 16in. tyres optional. 356A,B,C: 4.5J × 15 rims. 5.60 × 15in. tyres or 165 × 15in. 5.90 × 15in. or 185 × 15in. on Carrera.

Electrical equipment

Battery

6 volt

Dynamo
Bosch, mounted on cooling fan axis and driven by vee-belt from crankshaft pulley.
Ignition
Bosch, by single coil and distributor on pushrod engines. Two distributors and twin plugs on Carrera engines.
Starter motor
Bosch.
Headlamps
Bosch or Hella.

Dimensions for Coupé
Wheelbase: 2100mm/82.68in. (all models)
Front track: 1306mm/51.41in. (from 1952 – before then 1290mm/50.87in.).
Rear track: 1272mm/50.08in. (from 1952 – before then 1250mm/49.21in.).
Length: 4010mm/157.87in. (from 356B – before then 3950mm/155.51in.).
Width: 1670mm/65.75in. (from 356B – before then 1660mm/65.35in.).
Height: 1330mm/52.36in. (from 356B – before then 1220mm/48.03in.).
Weight: 935kg/2061.3lb. (from 356B – before then 720kg/1587.3lb.).

Production figures All models including Carreras

Type	Years	Prod.
356 Coupé	1950–55	6539
356 Cabriolet	1950–55	2139

356 Speedster	1954–55	1900

Total number of 356s: 10,578

356A Coupé	1955–59	13,007
356A Cabriolet	1955–59	3367
356A Speedster	1955–58	2922
356A Convertible D	1958–59	1330

Total number of 356As: 20,626

356B Coupé	1959–63	20,598
356B Cabriolet	1959–63	6194
356B Roadster	1959–62	2899
356B Hardtop	1961–62	1747

Total number of 356Bs: 31,438

356C Coupé	1963–65	13,509
356C Cabriolet	1963–65	3165

Total number of 356Cs: 16,674

356 series total production: 79,316

Distinguishing features through model years

1950
Bodywork
Two-piece split windscreen.
Integrated bumpers.
Front indicators below headlights, slightly inboard.
Rear lights placed vertically (rectangular above, round below).
Single aluminium grille, rear.
Small bonnet handle (no cut-out).
No sill (rocker panel) trim.
Rear side windows not hinged.
No vent windows in door glass.
Rear licence plate light with red brake light lens.
Interior
Three-spoke 'banjo' steering wheel.

Non-reclining seats.
Various configurations for rear seating (not standardised).
Two main instruments (speedo and tach or clock) plus oil temp gauge.
Indicator switch on top of dash in centre.
Wood door cappings.
Mechanical
1100cc engine.
4-speed 'crash' gearbox.
Cable operated drum brakes (cast iron drums).
$3\frac{1}{2} \times 16$in. wheels, same colour as bodywork.
Lever-arm shock absorbers.

1951
Bodywork
One-piece 'vee' windscreen.
Hinged 'pop-out' rear side windows.
Cut-out in bonnet handle.
Mechanical
1300cc engine introduced.
1500cc engine from October '51.
Hydraulic brakes.

1952
Bodywork
356A-style detached bumper introduced with aluminium over-riders.
Engine size script added at rear.
Interior
Reclining seats.
Standard rear seat with folding back (one-piece).
Indicator switch replaced by arm on steering column.
Tach made standard on all cars.

Mechanical
1500S engine introduced
October '52

1953
Bodywork
Front indicators directly below
headlights.
Two round tail-lights, side by side,
at rear.
Reversing light replaces brake light
in licence plate light assembly.
Interior
Two-spoke steering wheel with
Porsche crest in centre.
Metal door tops.
Mechanical
1300S engine introduced
November '53.
Synchromesh on all four gears.
Telescopic shocks at rear.
Aluminium brake drums.

1954
Bodywork
Horn grilles alongside front
indicators.
Interior
Steering wheel/knobs are ivory,
grey or beige colour.
Fuel gauge added.
Coupé interior light larger.

1955
Bodywork
Speedster introduced
September '54.
356A-style bonnet handle
introduced, with Porsche crest.
'Continental' badge added to some

Coupés and Cabriolets.

1956
Bodywork
356A introduced October '55 with
new curved windscreen, flat sill
panels (previously rolled-under)
and wide sill trim.
'European' script fitted to
some cars
Interior
Re-designed dashboard with three
main instruments (speedo, tach and
oil temp/fuel) and padded top.
Revised indicator switch and
handbrake.
Perforated vinyl headliner.
Mechanical
1600, 1600S and 4-cam 1500 Carrera
GS engines introduced (1500 and
1500S deleted).
Improved gearbox linkage and
3-piece aluminium casing (formerly
2-piece magnesium).
Anti-roll bar, uprated shock
absorbers and $4\frac{1}{2} \times 15$in metallic
silver wheels.

1957
Bodywork
Two teardrop-shaped rear lights
replace four round 'beehive' items
half-way through model year.
Rear licence plate light unit placed
beneath 'plate.
Re-designed door handles.
Chromed over-rider tubes added
on US-spec cars (split at rear
halfway through model year).
Mechanical
ZF steering box

1958
Bodywork
Convertible D replaces Speedster
August '58 (taller windscreen and
wind-up windows).
Removeable hardtop option on
Cabriolet which now features vent
windows in doors, altered rear
cowling and larger rear window.
Exhaust pipes exit through bumper
over-riders, except on Carrera.
Front indicators mounted on
wedge-shaped base.
Door striker plate lower and
secured by three screws (five
screws before).
Interior
Revised door panels.
Seats narrower and pleating pattern
changed.
Ash tray now located beneath das
Interior lights moved to sides in
Coupé.

1959
Bodywork
Higher front over-rider tube on
US-spec cars.

1960
Bodywork
356B introduced September, 1959
Front and rear end metalwork re-
designed incorporating larger,
higher bumpers, raised headlights
and larger, chromed bonnet handl
Coupé also receives vent window
Porsche script discontinued at
front.
Small grilles beneath front bumpe
Licence plate lights mounted on

rear bumper, with reflectors below or on pods above rear lights (US cars).
Narrower sill trim.
Roadster replaces Convertible D.
Interior
Black steering wheel, knobs, etc.
Shorter, chromed gear lever.
Individual cushions and folding backs in rear seating area.
Mechanical
1600 S–90 and 1600 Carrera GS engines introduced (2000 Carrera GS replaced 1600 GS in '62).
Modified transmission case, improved linkage.
Finned aluminium brake drums.

1962
Bodywork
Taller windscreen, larger rear window and engine lid on Coupé.
Squared-off front bonnet.
Two vent grilles on rear lid.
Fuel filler on right hand front wing.
Vents on front cowl (except Roadster).
Removeable rear window on Cabriolet.
Production of Roadster and Karmann Hardtop (introduced 1961) discontinued.
Badges at rear: 'Porsche 60' (1600cc, 60bhp engine), 'Porsche S' (1600 S) or 'Porsche 90' (90bhp 1600) or 'Carrera 2'.

1963–4
Bodywork
356C introduced July, 1963 (Coupé and Cabriolet only).

'1600 C' or '1600 SC' script at rear. Coachbuilders badges no longer fitted to right front wing.
Interior
Rubber grab handle replaces chrome item.
Console around ashtray.
Revised glove box.
Mechanical
Disc brakes front and rear.
Slightly different wheels with flat hubcaps.
1600 SC (95bhp) introduced July, 1963.

Authenticity check

Chassis and engine numbers through years

1950
356 Coupé 5002–5013, 5017–5018, 5020–5026, 5029–5032, 5034–5104, 5201–5410
356 Cabriolet 5001, 5014–5015, 5019, 5027–5028, 5033, 5105–5131

1100 engine 0101–0411

1951
356 Coupé 5411–5600
356 Cabriolet 5132–5162

1100 engine 0412–0999, 10001–10137
1300 engine 1001–1099, 20001–20821
1500 engine 30001–30737

1952
356 Coupé 11126–12084,

50001–50098
356 Cabriolet 10433–10469, 12301–12387

1100 engine 10138–10151
1300 engine 20822–21297
1500 engine 30738–31025
1500S engine 40001–40117

1953
356 Coupé 50099–51645
356 Cabriolet 60001–60394

1100 engine 10152–10161
1300 engine 21298–21636
1300S engine 50001–50017
1500 engine 31026–32569
1500S engine 40118–40685

1954
356 Coupé 51646–53008
356 Cabriolet 60395–60722
356 Speedster 80001–80200

1100 engine 10162–10199
1300 engine 21637–21780, 22001–22021
1300S engine 50018–50099, 50101–
1300A engine 21781–21999
1500 engine 32570–33899, 33901–34119
1500S engine 40686–40999, 41001–41048

1955
356/356A Coupé 53009–55000
356/356A Cabriolet 60723–61000
356/356A Speedster 80201–81900

1300 engine 22022–22273

1300S engine –50127, 50128–50135
1500 engine 34120–35790
1500S engine 41049–41999
1600 engine 60001–60608
1600S engine 80001–80110

1956
356A Coupé 55001–58311
356A Cabriolet 61001–61499
356A Speedster 81901–82580

1300 engine 22274–22471
1300S engine 50136–50155
1600 engine 60609–63926
1600S engine 80111–80756

1957
356A Coupé 58312–59090,
100001–102504
356A Cabrio' 61500–61892,
150001–150149
356A Speedster 82851–83691,
83792–84366

1300 engine 22472–22999
1300S engine 50156–50999
1600 engine 63927–66999,
67001–68216
1600S engine 80757–81199,
81201–81521

1958
356A Coupé 102505–106174
356A Cabriolet 150150–151531
356A Speedster 84367–84922
356A Convertible D 85501–
85886

1600 engine 68217–72468
1600S engine 81522–83145

1959
356A/356B Coupé 106175–108917
356A/356B Cabriolet
151532–152475
356A/356B Convertible D
85887–86830

1600 engine 72468–79999,
600101–601500
1600S engine 83146–85550

1960
356B Coupé 108918–114650
356B Cabriolet 152476–154560
356B Roadster 86831–88920

1600 engine 601501–604700
1600S engine 85551–88320
1600S-90 engine 800101–802000

1961
356B Coupé 114651–117476
356B Cabriolet 154561–155569
356B Roadster 88921–89483
356B Karmann Hardtop
200001–201048

1600 engine 88321–89999,
604701–606799, 606801–607750
1600S engine 085001–085670,
700001–701200
1600S-90 engine 802001–803999,
804001–804630

1962
356B Coupé 117601–121099,
210001–210899
356B Cabriolet 155601–156999
356B Roadster 89601–89846
356B Karmann Hardtop

201601–202299
1600 engine 607751–610000
1600S engine 701201–705050
1600S-90 engine 804631–806600

1963
356B/356C Coupé 121100–123042,
123304–125239, 126001–128104,
210900–214400, 215001–216738
356B/356C Cabriolet
157000–158700, 159001–159832

1600 engine 610001–611200,
600501–600600
1600S engine 705051–707200,
700501–701200
1600S-90 engine 806601–807400,
800501–080100
1600C engine 710001–811001,
730001–731102
1600SC engine 810001–811001,
820001–820522

1964
356C Coupé 128105–130511,
216739–219069
356C Cabriolet 159833–160750

1600C engine 711871–716084
1600SC engine 731103–733027,
811002–813562, 820523–821701

1965
356C Coupé 130512–131930,
219070–222579
356C Cabriolet 160751–162175

1600C engine 716085–
1600SC engine 733028–, 813563–,
821702